W0017814

Little
Palace

ADAM J. GELLINGS

STEPHEN F. AUSTIN STATE UNIVERSITY PRESS

Copyright ©2022 Stephen F. Austin State University Press

All rights reserved. Printed in the United States of America. No part of this book may be used or reproduced in any manner whatsoever without the writer's permission except in the case of brief quotations in critical articles or reviews.

For more information:
Stephen F. Austin State University Press
P.O. Box 13007 SFA Station
Nacogdoches, Texas 75962
sfapress@sfasu.edu
www.sfasu.edu/sfapress

Managing Editor: Kimberly Verhines
Book Design: Mallory LeCroy
Cover Photo: Adam J. Gellings
Distributed by Texas A&M Consortium
www.tamupress.com

ISBN: 978-1-62288-926-6

CONTENTS

3.

4.

Prompt

Write a poem about a character who goes for a walk at the beginning of autumn. Make it a clear afternoon. Have this character walk twelve blocks. One line per block. Let his eyes describe each object he passes. Show your readers what he has gained or lost along the way. Let his mind wander as quickly as his feet. A forgotten train in which people are still traveling. A sigh passing. A door that never closes. Remember—show your readers, don't tell. Hold still as you try your hand describing the prints of famous watercolors plastered to the bus stop. The Ferris Wheel under construction. The face of the auguste clown gesturing at the camera. Match it, color for color. Consider the little leaves. Consider the wind so gentle. Consider its early autumn song. Consider adding a quote from Cocteau as an epigraph. Let your pen slip. Let it sink in to where the sun is very strong, & where the shadows, very pale—lengthen. Vanish them. Act as though your character recognizes the gentleman sitting alone on a bench on the quay of the Seine, tossing fresh bread to a swan. Have the man use the phrase, "After me, the flood." Give him a name. Take a deep breath. Start each line off with

Because
because

1
[An Opening]

Airplane Mode

Touching clouds now. A tapestry of turned
& twisted. They are scarce & they are many.
One tries to be gentle, but this white space

serves only as a reminder that we are moving.
Above the light reflecting off the wing. Above
the dizzying display. The thought that I was good

with unrelenting dread. With the fallacy of falling
through an exit door. Not true. How darkness scatters
for a moment like droplets of water, warms

then rises again. Not letting anything through. Not
the sea. Not the cliffs. Not the tiny thatched roofs
of houses dolloped along the countryside. Somewhere,

they are looking up at us. Calling out names. *Cotton, cauliflower,
cumulous.* They are shutting windows. They are saying,
come inside now, dumpling. It's beginning to look like rain.

Fillet

From the base of my chin down
to pectoral fin, I am opened into

by the tip of the blade. Sequined flecks,
sharpening stone, shaved pieces of cobalt

& silver. The fat hands of the monger taking
my last bubbles of breath. That feeling

of a left hand cupping, cracking my cavity,
disappears. I'm good for you. I'd even

cross the salty pinks & reds of an ocean
to find you. Life was so simple. Now,

in the open air, on the warm white surface
of the operating table, I look confused.

My heart, like an old snail, is not the same
heart it once was. A shell of myself,

my eyes, my open mouth—now just a body
of light left on the table. Underneath it all,

the only four cats in town, bobbing, circling,
chasing their shadows.

The Father

When you are on your walk down Boulevard Saint-Michel, under that crowded gray sky, you will be the one to notice them. On your right, a pile of pink petals. The shadow of the gigantic double doors. A group of bicycles leaning together like drunk friends. You will snap a photo of them—then hold out your hand to see if it has begun to rain. The city workers will be cleaning the streets. You will see a group of teenage girls in stockings & pleated skirts brushing up against a black iron gate, looking very chic as they roll cigarettes. Not far off a carpenter will be doing his duties. He will not talk to you. He won't even look at you as he shaves & routes his precisions. He is a smoker, as all carpenters are. But do not bother him. Instead, take notice of the middle-aged man running into traffic, embracing an older man he will refer to only as *Père*. Their smiles will be identical. Watch as the younger man straightens the older man's flat cap. Watch as the younger man plants a kiss on both sides of the older man's cheeks. Then watch, as he slides his arm tightly up & underneath the older man's arm as they begin to exit the traffic circle. At this time, directly in front of *la fontaine du bassin Soufflot*, a vehicle will approach the small intersection. This shouldn't alarm you. It will swerve smoothly to the right of these gentlemen & you will remain perfectly still as the charm of goldfinches lifts from the white branches nearby & plunges into the half-light.

Le caquet

A large group of women

      all talking at once,
          off we go
               from voice to voice

   carrying the sound
of
grumble & matter
   wine & husbands   *(false messieurs)*

     grande engines
that overflow & overlap.

They wave over. *Come here!* they say.
              They say
        the soup is cold.
      They ask   again

the word

     for *thirst.*

Past Life

I buy a light, water repellent jacket
at The King of Frip vintage shop on the corner,
just as the sun is closing its doors.

The silence: a straight line
through the neighborhood, I notice   a hole
at the bottom of an unstitched pocket.

As I move,
something heavy starts to stir
in the thin lining that traces itself
along the clef of my elbow.

Come out, I say.
But how? How
do I tease you from the furthest corner? Hidden
in the edges
like a ghost   passing
            through a dream.

                         How, the size of you,
wider than a coin, sinking now
to my wrist.
How
        do I get you
                up
to my shoulder,
persuade you   to drop
down the long
back black of the jacket & come to rest
easily in the pouch
beneath the tattered hem...

I walk for a few blocks
whirling my arm like the windmill
above the *Moulin de la Galette,*
sifting rain as it skims over the surfaces of me,
turning gardens

into gardens.

Now I feel you, trying
trying —you are near—jostled, just
to the right   & there   lifted. Shining!

You are:
a single, gold earring, in the shape of V
for Valentino—inscribed on your spine.

Are you alone? How long
have you been hoping to see a reflection?
A friend?
To be held in a passing palm. I wonder,
as I picture the two of them,

the only two people on an empty street
the night sky full of stars they know
the words stopping in the middle of the dark:

Hold these——she says. A moment,
unclipped, hand-to-hand, then
arms linked again, returning
together

to this past life,
to this empty street, where it is still raining,
where it is still.

Palm
/pɔm/

I have learned

           to hold a palm in my hand.
For once I was right
where it landed when it fell.

           To cherish its heart-
shaped cascade of red knuckles round,
who waited for the advent of another.

           To let fingerprints glide
over purplish grubs tunneling deep
through watery flesh.

Almost touching in the bitter. Mouths
working endlessly
           to splinter this blossom

    in two.

Chemin Vert

I'm always one green light away
from wandering off the curb.

A promenade through the piercing
of crossed paths. I might've been

wrong when I said rainfall
follows my footsteps

at an angle. It starts off slow—
it gets quiet. In one way,

it cuts. But what journey am I on,
now that night has folded,

now that the cars
have turned on their headlights

for someone
I've only just imagined?

Guests

They arrived
precisely at seven. Saturday evening.
Happy faces. It was quiet. Nobody spoke
until one of them asked,
"Have you any cups?" They were fed
cocktails. They chewed
through the room. "I work
as a teacher" one said. "Who
are your lawyers?" one asked.
"My sister is a lawyer!" one yipped.
"My husband is a conductor" one said.
"To me, the idea of family sometimes feels all too tragic" one yawned.
The priest drank wine. I shimmied
around them like a rabbit through barbed wire.
A body on fire. I was friendly.
Tarts were served in the shape
of pickled hearts. A short man
grappled with grapes at the entrance of a long corridor. Somewhere
a Buddhist monk became a martyr. This,
it turns out
was foreshadowing.
"We live in extreme danger!' one said.
"Yes!" one said
Yes! everyone said. They all nodded.
There was a great toast. The cat cried out
like a gull. They proceeded at once to flood the doorway like rain
flooding an empty run-off
& soon
everyone had left
without saying goodbye.

Saturday 14 July, Champs de Mars

Even in the early afternoon
the crowd is thick & far reaching.
They've gnarled themselves around trees.
Stunted the spotlights of sun on the grass.
A chorus of blues & reds humming in unison
as the light begins to die.
I close my eyes
to the sound of hands joining
& search for a word that implies
the letting go of one's self.
When I open them
the sky has the look of a tomato
ripened, picked then wrapped loosely in newspaper.
As the firing squad begins to close in to smash it all open
we find a spot closer
to the brink of darkness.
Over our shoulders
Aida Garifullina scales smooth
the bel canto of *Casta Diva* & one fuse seems to ignite
another as the tower becomes
a choreographed panache of tricolor.
We are beachgrass at the swell of an ocean.
Cuticles on the fringes of a living breathing giant
lying on its back chanting *allez les bleus*.
& when it is all over, we choose our steps carefully
as we cross through borders
of garland
huddled like penguins
together by the hundreds
of thousands.
Are you getting a picture
of that endless channel of people

stretching the in-betweens of night, black with dye?
As we worm with them
through botanicals
covering the ground with our footprints
like oil on canvas,
we somehow manage
to break free from the torso of procession.
& it is right here that I mean to tell you
how much better your sight is than mine
how if you were to turn around just now
while the moon is showing her silver crescent
even from this great distance,
how you can still see them—
the slender embers of midnight falling
like strands of melisma
heavy enough to strike down the last train of a clock
on a night out of time.

Ghazal: La Belle Équipe

The chit-chat of cats through a crack in your window,
breaks with day past the edge of the window.

Bluets & peonies along rue de Charonne, sing
bouquet duets in full bloom of the windows.

& morning, it bends like notes of a sparrow,
to a crowd gathered large outside two double windows.

Notice how flames from candles can blur,
as memorials build to the sill of the windows.

Policemen patrol with sub-machine guns
(the steady Berettas' slight glare off the window)

while people recite names of innocent victims,
push roses through holes in panes of the windows.

Ruin

It was not as if they didn't try
to escape. Over fragments of amphitheater
in the heart of the city, a panoply

of flames turned to silence.
The sun on the spider
of stonework emerging like light

from the green grass. Just listen
when I tell you, there was once enough
black smoke to smother an entire

white sky. It was not as if they didn't think
to climb out. Over thick stone,
a courtyard of children humming

the final notes to a broken song.
Ruin the image of smoke curling their lips.
Ruin the moss clinging to the edge

of the column. Ruin the fierce winds that reached
for the bodies of first born, hand-rolled
& dropped into the thaw of an early grave.

The Two Margots

I am the swollen jaws of the sky

       exhaling into darkness.

I am the sequined hand grenade
tossed under a moon white

slowly breaking open—

       the field of blossoms burning.

Catacomb Poem

By noon
      we had reached the entrance
an assembly of limbs
chatting dimly   on the cusp

I took out my camera
fast-forwarded to where
we couldn't see
three steps ahead

     & stopped
where once there had been   all smiles
eyes   a smear of light
across my shirt
still warm
         though we dropped
like cogs into a big machine
unable
     to feel our way

For Security Purposes

We ask that you answer a few questions to confirm who you are
        for example
                when was your last
                transaction

Which is your favorite dessert
who is your favorite actress
what is your favorite board game

       whose side are you on

            anyway

Who is your favorite person from history
        can you think of anyone
                  more or less
                     American

How do you reach people
that don't trust anything Other

At what age did you first enter
      a foreign country
          (example –18)
          at what age were you first denied/
                  detained

Have you seen this
Would you stand up to that
              how long did it take you to cross
              the desert
              by foot
              or the Mediterranean

                    by wooden boat
                    with three hundred & fifty
                    Others

                at what time of day did your oldest child
drown (rounded

                to the closest hour for example)

Did you notice how low the horizon was
                did you refuse to sink
                    did you actually drink

                                        sea water
Which is your favorite desert

Did you ever report what happened to you
                at the camp
                did it sound
                        like a windstorm
            in the back of your throat

Did they cup you
                in their hands

                        did you make noises
                            squirm

                            move around

Did it ever make you wonder

                        why now

What street did your best friend live on before
                    the airstrikes turned her

                                entire family
                into a sunburst of atoms   orbiting
                            un-chambered   undone

how many years did this take
off of your own life expectancy

What was your oldest sibling's nickname
                                    & was it a swift amputation

                                 & did you think
                                 that every soft molecule
                                 of a nurse
                                 comes from the stars

                         was it worth trying
                         to save him
                         were you relieved
                         it wasn't you

What is the name of the university
                               your spouse attended
                     & who was their rival
                              was it rebel held East or
                     government held West

                     & since you've arrived

                     has anyone made you feel
                               as though
                     all your passwords have expired.

2

[Some Aspects of Paris Life]
[The Bonnard Exhibition]

Avenue du Bois de Boulogne

On a dirt path
the shadows of pigeons crossing sky
beneath them
the loose, supple wings
of heraldic lilies blue
& wet
or the ant on this green wooden bench
waving antennae.

Street Seen from Above

The windows open
& the dry fabric of sky moving
in & out.

All day long,
the voices of Vespas drag
like slow burns.

      They spend their lives
with backs to the sun,
never looking up.

Carrying with them a burden
of unspeakable sound
emerging

        through coughs of exhaust.

      To the supermarket
to find what they think they need
for dinner.

Long after dark,
they hurry home,
prodding at the underswirl

of traffic, alone—
thirsty for a life
      other than theirs.

House in the Courtyard

With my eyes closed

in the blue of each morning, I find

there is no desire within me

to leave this bed. I can hear

a bottle breaking.

Below a hose is splashing

against concrete. A thousand

jasmine flowers renew,

renew.

Boulevard

It's the end of the week.
The fish on ice look opaque & heavy.
The clams peek through the cracks
of their harsh little worlds.
The dog lands a bone & settles
where there is shade but no breeze.
The bell of Saint-Paul Saint-Louis
extols its holy oath to the people
waiting for falafel.
There you are! she says
as she steps outside the boutique
taking the hand of the boy.
He raises his head & smiles.
He is too young to know
she won't always be there.

Street Corner

There is a man who likes the taste of olives.
He is scuffling all over the street.
He is smudging his face squinting into the sun.
All of this heat he is saying to himself.
Now he is turning the key to a small apartment.
He is unlocking a bottle of wine.
Now the cork is lifting, the way a blackbird lifts
from the sidewalk. A cherry in its beak
                                        awakened.

Street Corner Seen from Above

From here, the street vendor's song
goes something like a three note bird call
echoing off the grey roofs & the red chimneys
over the small dark figures walking hand-in-hand
where *Les Halles* market used to be.

The Square at Night

How the wind drags a column
of tobacco smoke
just to startle the air
just to feel alive
just
to see itself
ripple
against the shimmering splash
of taillights
where it lingers
for awhile
like a face
scratched into the surface
of the moon
until night claims it
as one of us.

The Pushcart

She moves among the maze of vendors, over stone-paved streets, a
rupture of crackling, one wheel always a bit broken, stumbling, then
steady, passing like the slow exhale of accordion, time & again, when
no one is watching, a few tumble to her feet, fracturing their skulls,
she stops for a moment, surveys for survivors, draws them close,
gives them a kind of warmth, pearls on a vine, a pleasure rarely tasted,
arranging their bruises with the softness of her years, she bends
forward at the hip, lifts the life of colors with her thick hands & starts
again, as the morning sun begins to warm in the open air, the smell of
crêpes, the pigeons like small cranes, ants plundering for blood in the
cracks, flies gushing on.

The Street at Night in the Rain

I heard a call through the rain. I heard it ring & ring & ring. I answered it; listened a long time for the words to reveal themselves. All night long, anonymous shapes found safety beneath an awning. In the shadows, running down a windowpane, even the electric glow of light flowed into the street.

At the Theater

There was a heroine who wiped pebbled sweat from her brow.

Sweethearts who stuffed the front rows & whispered
    not a word.

An anxious child who turned, turned
    in his seat

& a mother who brought his chatter to a close.

There were shadowy curtains that swept
    & lights that began to flower

the long hours of night
    into a dusty new maroon.

The Bridge

1.

I want to rest where the driftwood gathers.
So I slide off my shoes & sit
along the bank. My feet
dangle
over the patterns of ripples & twirls.
Silhouettes cross

above a rising wind. Sunset
thins to a sirens cry
before breaking off
into a cloud. Somewhere,
a guitar & the faint stream
of harmonica swing through the air
like fishhooks.

2.

Every inch
of the boat cruise is covered
in people. They point & they wave
in layers as they glide past.
Cameras out,
shifting upward
above beckoning bodies.

The *click – click – click*
of heels on the walkway
as a woman approaches, looks
over my shoulder to see what it is
I am sketching.   But these,
I show her,
are just words.

3
[Selections of Drawings and Prints]
[Stained-Glass Windows]
[Watercolors]

Claude Monet, *Argenteuil*, 1875

It was a lot of things.

It was the algae blooms swimming against the tide.

It was the convent of masts, making partial signs
of the cross
across the sky's chest.

The eyes & brow suspended in clouds passing.

You could almost feel the dew on the nose
of the bows
                    quivering.

                                        I know the sun,
tinged red, sat somewhere above the blue, burning
into the day.

*

It was a thousand miles ago,
& now I can only imagine
those deep December nights in Ohio.
Selling the house. Coming to visit you, frail
& fevered pressing your cold hands together & together
watching the dancers across the street
in the one room studio.

Each night, the same couple
curving over the hardwood, knees bent   bending
lead & follow, chest to chest, smooth
                            then slow   slow.

43

I think of the night you whispered
how you wanted just one more
summer. Just one more chance to see the geese
floating through the ravine. The deer
in the middle of the rain-kissed leaves.

The tiny Monet postcard in white frame on the nightstand.
"I'd like to go *there*," you said. Your hand crumpling
around a tissue.

*

Calls were made. Come now.
Come get your goodbyes. Come touch
each light blue bead of the rosary with us,
passing it gently
through the calm of our fingers.

*

That night,
I stepped outside onto the wet black brick of the patio,
blew smoke
        under the glow of the yellow bulb & noticed him

across the street, locking the front door of the studio.
                                        He turned,

looked me in the eyes
offered a short nod as I stood
still as a fawn
scarved in the steam of its own breath.

The snow staring back into us
like white on a cloud.

Daguerreotypes

The country couple
sitting with hands folded
peppered in flashpoints.

Or their young child
who remains still
just long enough

for dusty spoonfulls
of exposure to burst
through a smoky mirror.

There is his voice
shining in mid-flight.
Reaching for the end

of a long white ribbon
on the strong head
of the silent woman.

Her smile
is like a hairline fracture
in the middle of a 7

that finishes the end of a year
like some hard winter
finishes the stone gazes

on a row of gothic statues,
frozen in daylight
& forgotten

under silver-bellied blankets
of snow.

Autoportrait

Do you recognize me? Let the eyes
settle. Let them become careless

without cause. Without reason,
I have become lost

in any song that comes my way.
In my home, in the ashes

that remain, I have moved
past the feeling of wanting

to be cracked open. Too afraid
to go back.

How could I make it through & to
the end?

All my life I have waited to be shown
where it is safe to hide

this body. Keeping a little mantle glowing
in the darkest parts of the forest.

I have resized this frame a hundred different ways.
Let me show you

the crusade of monarch butterflies spiraling out
from their crown of shyness.

Moving all things.
The resurrection of birdsong.

Learning to hunt,
above the blow of the badlands & blue thistles.

Above
where even the trees avoid touching.

Triptych of a father by his son

1. *Profile on a pale background*

Here

      the figure is placed
at the head of the table   projected

      above all else

2. *Hands that break bread*

      in the absence of light:

he is a dab of pearl gray

shivers on his face
      skin of memory

he is crying out: *Make me what I want to be*

3. *From across the room*

eyes that seem to follow
      wherever you go

they are
you are

stone   stem of red-ginger

the contour of gentle hills
painted over

L'Amour fou

after Pablo Picasso's *'Portrait de Marie-Thérèse'*

Perched like a parrot against the cold grey mono-
chrome of a discarded urn, you arrived

after a bluish period. Smooth, shell-colored skin
sculpted from summers at the beach, cloudy

pale eyes like early smoke rising
above the busiest Saturday night on rue de Lappe.

In the easy streets & easel-sized quarters of Paris you crossed
paths outside the doors of the Galeries Lafayette, first

words that sealed your fate: *Mademoiselle, you have
a very interesting face. I would like to do a portrait of you.*

I am Picasso.

You never passed as the gardener's wife.
Never posed outside the edges of the tormented

canvas. Burnished in bourgeois bronze & scaled down,
you were only eyes; only eyes between legs, only

legs holding arms & arms holding on
to the teenage heart of *la femme enfant.*

From my vantage point, in the hall across the large,
open gallery, you are a bowl of fruit in a room

of white silhouettes. So still, that once
I tried to touch the hollow sockets of your lachrymose

nose, tried to picture your outline, so pure, spinning
head first from the rafters of an empty garage.

A wreath of flowers, withered in the autumn
of South France, far from the backdrop of chic

summers & striped suits. A life worth so much more
than the flick of the finger he raised to call you

complete.

Watercolor

& now there is no blue,
        forget the clouds
pushing the night
        into the red sun,

the hill
        alive with the crunch
of dead leaves.
        When I was a boy,

I painted a path for us
        to follow
down a frozen shoreline,
        bright enough

to pull you.
        We followed it
like candlelight, winding
        from canvas

to open canvas.
        One night,
we listened for the call
        of the magpie,

a pearl thief,
        among the panoramic
freeze & waited
        while the weeping

willows pitied themselves.
        The shores beneath
their frames
        pitted

by the empty
        shells of snails.
When we emerged,
        you noticed

I no longer knew
        how to paint a hand
reaching out
        for an orange—

or how flowers,
        a tapestry of peonies,
seemed to lay
        suspended inside me.

Soon,
        your own face
began to blur, your skin
        faded before me, white

as the body
        of Séverine,
so white,
        I wondered

if you were ever there.
        This pigment of doubt
hanging
        inside me

for a moment
        like the sun,
so high,
        that searching

for the missing pearl
        from your necklace
became
        obsolete.

Impression I (In lieu of)

Once
in the middle
of a long furrow, I stood
firm, too shallow
to hide. I felt the shape
of the plow covering
my blisters, suckling earth.
Which dream is this? I asked
the fine lines that kept me
like palm groves
under snow. A buried coin,
fool's gold. I was
memorizing lines
on colored marble, a forgery
of a poem in stone
that for many years
I had succeeded
in trying to forget.

Impression II

I invented a mother

She was coming out from behind a patch of open timber

How she stood with her young at the edge of a creek bed

Come closer I thought

It happened in the middle of the body

It happened in real time, the sound

The breaking spine of an old book

There was a wound that blazoned like lights on a grotto

There was a wound that never appeared

Impression III

In the dream, it seemed everyone had grown older,
                              but I remained the same

clump of earth, taxidermied bird.
                              It took me a lifetime to see the sun

shining through a rain shower. That is to say, unclouded.
                              That is to say look

    how it glistens now   kind orb,

round heavy head of the martyr,   look now

                              how it courts the eye

Au Bar D'hôtel

Thursday night

Earlier,
you removed the vacation photos,
smoking Marlboro Lights
on the terrace, too occupied

to panic. You spoke long before
bedtime. Did not hesitate to say sweet words,
just discovered. Some words

do not veil their faces. They tell you
one thing—what you wish from the heart,
an ending you can understand.

People coming out
in the 6th arrondissement.
On a niche, half of Paris

has already seen you
take a deep breath. In the smoking room,
time passes. Makes you forget

your day, your very best day.
The horizon doing it right.
You take a drink.

Untitled (The Largest Room in the Salon)

It's a naked woman
pouring a pitcher of water
over another naked woman
s t r e t c h I n g
across a canvas.

It's a lot of small dots,
up close.

It's a lion hunt,
far away.

It's a canary feeding
on a nipple,
then breaking free
from the wall
with a throat full of milkweed.

It's a beautiful, beautiful dress
assembled from everything
you've ever wanted
to touch.

It's the perfect rose, chipping
like a rose.

The hollowed ring
of a musket.   The head

splitting open

at just the right angle.

To you

This is a bleuet
& I'll bring it to you—the trembling dark,
greyish green stem.

They are all around you,

but there is only one

hidden in the canyon
of your eye

& I'll bring it to you.

Bonaparte Crossing the Alps

after Paul Delaroche's *'Bonaparte franchissant les Alpes'*

Surely, you are not thinking about how poorly
This will all end one day. Does Elba even exist
On an isolated trail through the Alps in May?
Your mule already looks downtrodden. It moves.
It's alive. The icicles are silent.
These boulders enjoy the company, I'm sure.
Don't let them push you around.
Consider the gusts of wind
A welcoming gesture,
Kisses to your frosty cheeks.

There are easier routes to lead 40,000 men
Twisting, carrying heavy artillery.
There are warmer waist-coats to hide
A little corporal's hand inside.

But no one would dare question the young
First Consul of the Republic. Hold on
To your bicorn & march to the rising
Drumrolls thundering along the difficult
Descent, framing a labyrinthine
Passage towards victory.
Martial flutes soar up
To that little bit of blue that peeks through
A whitewashed sky.

Perhaps a change of weather is in store, but today
There is wind in the Alps, freezing
Your afternoon gaze.

4

[Post-Impressionists]
[The Retrospectives]
[Miniatures]
[Café]

A Father's Day Card for the Elephant of the Bastille

> *"It was an elephant, forty feet high, constructed of timber*
> *and masonry, bearing on its back a tower which resembled*
> *a house, formerly painted green by some dauber, and now*
> *painted black by heaven, the wind, and time."*

Victor Hugo, *Les Misérables*

The Elephant of the Bastille
carried you on his back.
He threw the baseball with you even
when his shoulder was bothering
him. He gave you extra attention.
Your first pocket knife.
The loose change from the cracks of his belly.

For many years you walked away from
his mouldering tusks. You called on Sundays.
You didn't want to acknowledge the holes
in his plaster. The rats picking away
his weakening insides. The street urchin
taking up residence inside one of his legs.

Your mother tried keeping him together
for as long as she could. Picking up
the crumbling pieces & pasting them back together.
No passer-by offered to help.
No longer was he the roaring symbol
of strength lifting you up with his trunk
toward the sky.

He moved
through the end of his life
slow as a stone passing along the bottom

of the Seine. A still life with chair.
A shrine whose bronze cast simply
never arrived.
             Too soon,
he belonged to the night.

But this is just a note to say
you're thinking of him today,
from your seat inside the bistro
             next to the mouth
of the canal.

Your view slightly obscured
by the June rain tossing itself against the window—
a boundless sky,

      such heavy rain.

The Egg

sizzles in its skillet.
I wait

with my legs crossed
at the kitchen table.
The sun
gives its burning attention
to an empty chair. The cat
wanders over,

licks my big toe, returns
to her spot
on the carpet

filled with morning.

Little Palace

Outside the bar a neon arrow flashes. Inside,
a group of gauche maquettes struggles to fit
perfectly together in their stools; weighted, shifting,
cackling open. Tonight, everyone here feels like
royalty—crocheted into the crest of a fleur-de-lis.
Sunset dies behind a crowd of carriages rusting
in the street, but it's never too late to press play
on the juke. Bone to bone. Fingerlings hissing
in oil. Part voice. Part scotch. A sacred space,
where magic is played on a broken arcade. The
jugular of the juggler. Sweat running down the faded
blue of his neck tattoo. Rushing to find some air.
Shallow pools gather under the plinth of cool drafts.
Shots fired. Bottles of smoke set free, disappear.

In the Argentinean Restaurant

The window is cracked & you
are just a name carved
into the table.

Some days I can feel it,

the tallest letter
spreading through my fingers.

Outside,
the sun has this trick
of spinning in the air,

blue birds settle on a fence line.

Their talk blankets my sighs,
I'm told

each one is different.

Song Without Words

Rue Lamarck, Montmartre

The afternoon shuttles through the city.

Faces stride like dancers
in the fresh air.

Windows are open
the sun is out.

I notice you
under the rose
red awning of the flower shop

floating past
the abundance
of cream
apricot
lime green
light blue   cloud blue   blooming.
Your name

lumps in my throat. A bony stem
trying to pass a whisper
through a language I should know.

It's early June.
For a few hours I sit & watch the sun
light up a tree line. The wind

whips at its leaves, chasing them
down a spiraling green alley
that curves

like a tongue.

Maria Callas at the Paris Opera House, May 29, 1965

Ah, be once more as you were.
When I first gave my heart to you.
—Norma

The moon shines through a thick tremble of trees

Her stone cold profile in grainy black & white

Against the glow of the orchestra pit

A version of a swan begins to unfold

She swathes through the catcalls & whistles

With outstretched arms that ache to be flowered

One man lurks inside the shadows for her return

One man left her waiting on the sharp edges of an alter long ago

The way she almost sank the knife into him

A chill of indifference down the stroke of her back

She rolls a roulade through a wound

Beneath the immaculate white of the costume she wears

Cadenzas scatter like ash in the garden

A range of stresses that shatter the nerves

She collapses at the bend in a long breath

A low moan exits the doors of L'Opera like a prayer

One man crosses himself with fingers outstretched

One man crosses himself with fingers bunched together

The women toss flowers from their hair

Laurel leaves linger around the crown

For a moment they feel the intensity of the flame

But it was always there   burning like this

The Artist's Father, Reading *"L'Événement"*
Paul Cézanne, 1866

On the edge of his oversized seat. Unsympathetic. Rigid, the way a lozenge waits impatiently in the heart of a throat—for it to be over. As if even the loudest noise, perhaps knocking at the front door, couldn't disturb his disinterest. In this way, he looks unfinished. Looked down upon. The slightest unease of a squint, asking *Who reads this junk anyway?* Though resigned to hanging the small still life that rests on the wall above his shoulder; he doesn't understand it. He sees pears one way: *as pears*. Don't try convincing him otherwise. As he drifts now, in & out of sleep, it becomes time to soften the harder lines of flesh. To narrow the distance between a son's easel & his father's favorite chair. He begins to tilt to one side. Heavy, the paper that fills the space inside his stiff, carved-like hands, always searching

for what isn't there.

Baguettes

Back at the flat on rue des Tournelles,
I place bread flour & salt

on the counter. Spool a little well
with my finger & crumble yeast

into its center, slowly. I pour
lukewarm water into the well

watching the yeast dissolve,
adding flour until the dough

becomes smooth & stretchy.
Push   push with the heel of my hand,

folding it back into itself,
folding it back

into itself. Until
it bounces & shines   bounces

& shines.

When I was twenty-two I dropped out of school to begin cooking in an Italian restaurant with my best friend, Morgan. The bread baker was a good friend of ours. His name was Jake. I was asleep the night he took his own life with a single shot from a twelve gauge, in a hotel near Hilltop. He was twenty-five. The next morning the owner of the restaurant asked if Morgan & I wouldn't mind taking over bread baking & pasta making. Despite the two us having no prior experience.

There are only four ingredients
in a baguette:

> flour
> water
> fresh yeast
> salt

> An actual law in France stipulates
> that a baguette will not legally be
> acknowledged as a baguette unless
> it contains these four ingredients.
> Around the time of King Louis XIV,
> baguettes were wide & clunky, rising
> on thick decks of steam ovens, often
> reaching a yard or two in length. Not
> until 1920, when a new law prevented
> bakers from working before 4 a.m. (thus,
> making it impossible for a large, round
> loaf to be ready in time for breakfast)
> did the baguette become the long, slim
> loaf we see sticking out from grocery
> bags, backpacks or tucked under arms
> hurrying home.

Each morning
Morgan & I would arrive at around 7 a.m.
to start prepping the dough.

The room was small.
The restaurant was dark & quiet
except for the steady hum of the mixer,
its wire whip fishtailing
in the large, stainless steel bowl.

Between him & I,
60 loaves per day
plus a tray of focaccia
& a medley of pasta & noodles.

The smell of Semolina
Rosemary Potato
Honey Wheat
or a simple round
Pagnotta country bread
were ours to choose.

After
letting the dough sit
for half-an-hour,
I give it a body.
Gently at first.
Cheekbones, with my thumb
& index finger pressing its round
waistline, sculpted
pale beneath my skin.
Satiny dusts of flour
to my hands
when they start to stick.
Pounding hard
to reshape it's center against
the snowy counter
until it's figure is full.
I'm relentless.
Kneading & stretching
inside-out
each time it reaches
for its perfect bloom.
Then, I divide
the dough into four
light, playful globes
& switch on the oven.
As the seconds pass,
I shape them into leg bones,
carefully,
with the undersurface
of my shadow-hand,
placing them on top
of the cooking tray to rest
& rise.

We called it the "Bread Room"
We plugged in our iPods
We cracked eggs
We mixed dough
We cut strips of pasta
We talked with the staff that dropped in
We wondered what the last song was Jake listened to
We wondered what was on TV when the trigger pulled
We wondered if his parents knew about his lover
We wondered who the last person was he talked to
We wondered
We said as much as we knew
We said as far as we knew
We waited
We stacked trays on a rack
We swept the floor
We got the lights
We closed the door

1.   When the oven has reached 250°C
                & the dough has doubled in size,
                the scarification process begins.

2.   Slash a slight angle
                about a quarter of an inch deep
                towards the top of the loaf.

3.   Now slash to the right of the first cut,
                & so on,
                down to the bottom of the dough.

4.   The overlapping slashes will expand,
                opening the shape of the bread
                in its early stages of baking.

5.   Slip a handful of ice cubes
                into the bottom of the small oven
                & place the baguettes on the middle rack.

                (The ice creates steam for the loaf to develop
                a golden, shiny crust)

After

After a few years at the Italian place. After I had left & went to manage the kitchen at a lousy chain-restaurant. After the dough was flown in frozen each Monday morning.

After two years there. After I decided it was probably time to go back to school. After the joy of baking lost its brightness with each passing day. After I had weathered out completely.

I keep an eye moving
        until they are ready

to come into the world.
        A gentle, *tap-tap*

on the bronze blush of their bellies—
        hollow, airy

the crackling of cooling bread
        being ripped apart.

Now

Now, it is night here.
I stare out from one of the two small windows
directly above the sink.

In my third story flat, around the corner
from Place des Vosges, I watch
as a woman dressed in all white, glacé gloves,

handbag, & her young son,
walk a dog so small it could fit between
the threads of my pocket.

Today, for a moment,
it felt like I was back
in the "Bread Room."
So I take a picture
with my phone of their thin

profiles & send it
to Morgan,
living in London now.
I title the message something witty—

Still got it

It takes a few minutes
but he responds
with an image of his own,
& with it

a message that leads me to pull out
one of the grainy wood chairs
from beneath the dining room table
& sit down.

I made a sourdough starter over the weekend & made this today. It's my first loaf in years.

[View Attachment]

I read it over

       & over

Arc de Triomphe

I am leaving a few bad thistles I know
behind.

I am certain they won't follow home
to my garden. Many colors,

my garden. So sweet & so hungry.
I thumb through its every lambs ear.

Its milky undertones. Its bees I find
I don't always understand. They hiss & they

hum to a halt. They are the sons of so on
& so on. They are not moths.

They are dumping their honey in yellow fields
outside the city.

Their queen, a stone pillar to which every
tree-lined procession arrives.

They knife blossoms into silence. They go on
& go on, perfectly forever

until all at once— against a kiss of wind,
                                they topple.

Back to Life

after Paul Cézanne's 'L'hermitage à Pontoise'

Grab the base of the tree trunk
& shake out
the different colors.

The lights inside a blue thatched roof
switch
       on
          to off.
The sleepy row of hedges
need pruning.

Who clips those sagging trees,
opens the windows
to a mid-summer's breeze?

Beneath a horizon floating
         over the edge of the woods,
the climbing light
            of midday follows

the cutting shadows
           into the quiet courtyard.

Listen
to the dying garden, whistling
at the base of the hillside.

Ask Pissarro to plow it.

Get him a handcart & a shiny
red spade. A cushion

for his knees.
Rub out the dead.

Plant a cascade of vibrant roses.
Call them beautiful.
Make them desperate for bee stings.

Deleted Scenes

Outside,
more fog. It has begun to rain. He slips
a thin cigar between his lips. She flicks
a cigarette & exhales a wad of cash from her bra,
sets it on a table full of black-eyed Susans.
He wipes dried blood with a napkin from his nose.
A swollen punch-line. She starts to undress, he looks
puzzled. There's talk of a boat ride that night
despite the weather. She slides off her rings
& washes his hair in the kitchen sink. Guides his head
under the running water. Her hands are warm.
She is a rising star. A femme fatale. He is a stuntman
on a white horse jumping stone fences in the dark.
Tell me something, she says.
What is it, he says.
Will they come for us?
Oh, he says,
              it's so hard to say.

Acknowledgments & Notes

Many thanks to the following journals for publishing earlier versions of these poems:

Atlanta Review, "A Father's Day Card for the Elephant of the Bastille"

DIALOGIST, "Prompt"

DMQ Review, "Impression I (In lieu of)" & "Impression III"

Glass: A Journal of Poetry, "For Security Purposes"

EcoTheo Review, "Claude Monet, Argenteuil, 1875"

The Ekphrastic Review, "Bonaparte Crossing the Alps"

Porridge, "Street Corner" & "Street Seen From Above"

Prelude, "Untitled (The Largest Room in the Salon)"

Quarter After Eight, "Watercolor"

Rise Up Review, "Ghazal: La Belle Équipe"

Ruminate, "Impression II" & "Palm"

The Saint Ann's Review, "House in the Courtyard"

South Bank Poetry, "Le caquet" & "The Father"

Summit Avenue Review, "In the Argentinean Restaurant"

The Tangerine, "Arc de Triomphe"

Willow Springs "Deleted Scenes"

"Back to Life" & "Song Without Words" originally appeared in the anthology *A Rustling and Waking Within: Poems Inspired by the Arts in Ohio*, published by Ohio Poetry Association Press.

————————

In "Prompt," the line "After me, the flood"; in French, "Après moi, le déluge" is often credited to King Louis XV of France, who himself, altered a version originally attributed to his lover, Madame de Pompadour, "Après nous, le déluge", or "After us, the flood."

"Ghazal: La Belle Équipe" was written in the aftermath of the attacks in Paris on November 13, 2015, that killed 130 people, including the deaths of 21 at La Belle Équipe restaurant in Paris's 11ème.

The poems in the second section take their titles from work in a series by French artist Pierre Bonnard (1867-1947) called "Some Aspects of Paris Life".

"Au Bar D'Hotel" uses only translated language found on page 71 of the magazine L'OFFICIEL Paris, June/July 2016.

"Song Without Words" is after the Jens Kongshammer painting *The Flower Sellers*, in collection at the Brandt-Roberts Galleries in Columbus Ohio.

I am grateful to Arianna Huffington's "Maria Callas: The Woman Behind the Legend" & John Ardoin's "Callas: The Art and the Life" & "The Callas Legacy", in which I heavily reference biographical information, operatic terms, language, & details of Callas' final performance as Vincenzo Bellini's *Norma* in Paris in 1965. The epigraph for the poem is taken from the end of Act 1 — Scene 4 of *Norma*.

This book would not be possible without the steadfast support of the following people:

My parents, Bev & Herm; the Mardulas; Angela, Paul, Derek, Lainey & Trevor; Gregory W. Cameron, Emily & Morgan Ferretti, the Tienprasids; Andrea, Anthony, Enzo & Gio, Heather & Jerry Tuvell.

Immense thanks & gratitude to Nora Alkhamis, Carla Barger, Cassie Brown, Matthew Robb Brown, shane carreon, Elizabeth Dark, Jen DeGregorio, Darren C. Demaree, Dante Di Stefano, Kristin Distel, Angie Estes, Jeroen Gerrits, Maria Mazziotti Gillan, Macaulay Glynn, Stephen Haven, Joe Hess, Leslie Heywood, Heather Humphrey, Meredith Janning, Negesti Kaudo, Carolyn Keller, Christian Lambrecht, Nathan Lipps, Kelly Neal, Kimberly Ann Priest, Bernadette Roe, Doug Rutledge, Pamela Smart, Karen Swortzel, Elizabeth "Libby" Tucker, Leah Umansky, Enikő Vághy & Joe Weil; for their focus, support & time spent with the poems in this manuscript.

To all of the students at SUNY Binghamton & the Binghamton Poetry Project that I had the pleasure to teach or workshop with, thank you.

I am indebted to Colleen Bailey, Donna Berg, Colleen Burke & Rose McNierney, for their care, generosity & kindness in helping me navigate through the PhD program at Binghamton. You each deserve more than just an acknowledgement in a book of poems for all that you've done for myself & for so many. Thank you, thank you.

Adam J. Gellings is a poet and instructor from Columbus, Ohio. He received his MFA from Ashland University and his PhD from the State University of New York at Binghamton, where he was the recipient of a fellowship from the Marion Clayton Link Endowment. His poems have appeared in numerous journals & magazines including *New South*, *Salamander*, *The Southamptom Review*, *Willow Springs* and elsewhere.

CPSIA information can be obtained
at www.ICGtesting.com
Printed in the USA
BVHW040900110922
646361BV00004B/25